DINO BUILDERS!
ABCs

Derek Alexandrenko

Aa

Articulated dump truck

Bb

Bulldozer

Cement truck

Dd

Drill

Ee

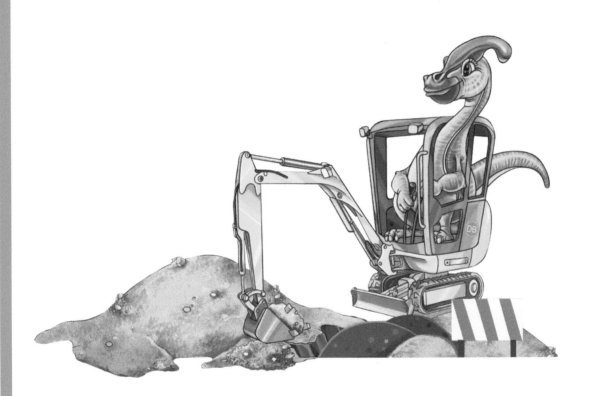

Excavator

Ff

Front loader

Grader

Hh

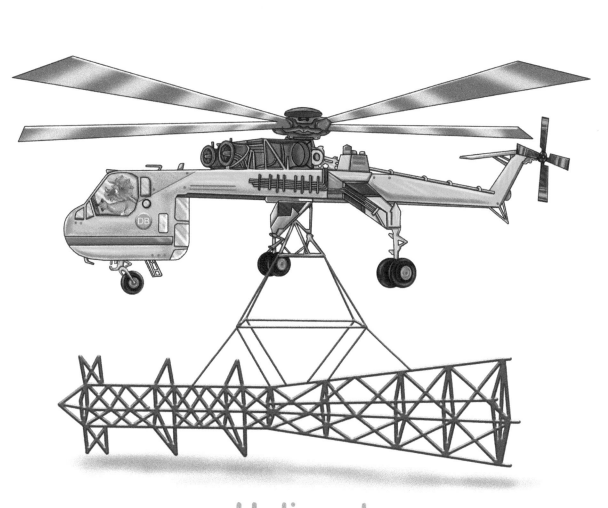

Helicopter

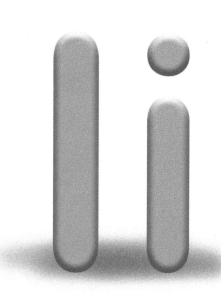

Impact wrench

Jack hammer

Kk

Knot

Ladder

Mm

Material handler

Nn

Nail gun

Offroad dump truck

Pp

Power trowel

Qq

Quarry rock drill

Rr

Road paver

Ss

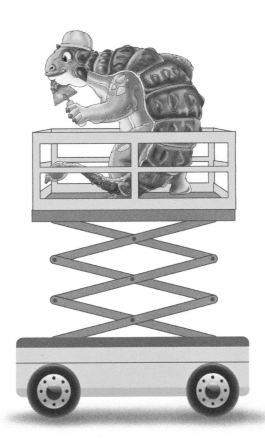

Scissor lift

Tt

Telescopic fork lift

Uu

Utility vehicle

Vacuum truck

Welder

X-ray machine

Yarder

Zz

Zamboni

CPSIA information can be obtained
at www.ICGtesting.com
Printed in the USA
LVHW070856230721
693494LV00007B/719

9 781736 329764